MEDITATIONS
ON THE
HOLY
ANGELS

MEDITATIONS
ON THE
HOLY
ANGELS

———

ST. ALOYSIUS GONZAGA

TRANSLATED BY

FR. ROBERT NIXON, OSB

TAN Books

Gastonia, NC

Translated by Fr. Robert Nixon, OSB

Cover design by Jordan Avery

Cover image: "Regina Angelorum", by William-Adolphe Bouguereau, 1900 (oil on canvas) / Wikimedia Commons.

ISBN: 978-1-5051-2633-4
Kindle ISBN: 978-1-5051-2634-1
ePUB ISBN: 978-1-5051-2635-8

Published in the United States by
TAN Books
PO Box 269
Gastonia, NC 28053
www.TANBooks.com

Printed in India

Meditations on the Holy Angels is part of the TAN Books series which includes old, timeless Catholic books that have been updated and now reprinted for your spiritual growth. Besides producing traditional Catholic content from living authors, TAN Books looks to the saints and spiritual masters of the past to guide us in the present and into the future to our true home, heaven. Meditations on the Holy Angels *was written by Saint Aloysius Gonzaga, who lived from 1568–1591.*

"For he shall give his angels charge over thee,
to keep thee in all thy ways.
They shall bear thee upon their hands,
lest thou dash thy foot against a stone."

—*Psalm 90:11–12*

CONTENTS

TRANSLATOR'S NOTE

DESPITE THE BREVITY of Saint Aloysius Gonzaga's life (1568–1591), he is one of the most dearly loved and widely venerated saints of the Society of Jesus. His achievements, if measured in purely earthly or secular terms, were admittedly very few. Yet during his brief twenty-three years of mortal life, he exhibited such charity, piety, purity, and fervor of devotion that he has served as a wonderful example and source of inspiration to a great multitude of the faithful over the centuries. Today, he is recognized and venerated as the patron saint of youth and students.

Although a great many books have been written about this popular saint in various languages over the centuries, it is not widely known that he himself was also a very promising author. His longest and most significant work is that which is offered in the following pages, for the first time in English, the *Meditations on the Holy Angels.* This fascinating and inspiring work reveals much about the saint's devotion to the angels as exemplars and protectors; indeed, his numerous biographers have consistently characterized the life and conduct of Aloysius himself as "angelic," indicating not only the heavenly character of his life and nature but also his intense devotion to the holy angels.

The source of the text of this work from which the present translation has been made is the 1850 Cologne edition of the *Opera Omnia Sancti Aloysii Gonzaga* edited by A. Heuser. The chapter divisions and titles have all been added by the present translator.

It is hoped that this translation of this unique and significant work by Saint Aloysius will not be of interest to scholars of Renaissance piety and religious thought only but also of value in promoting prayer and devotion to the holy angels, as the saint himself certainly intended. His literary approach is naturally underpinned by a solid foundation of Tridentine, Thomistic scholasticism but also infused with the fire of his own heartfelt piety and the spontaneity and imagination of youth. This is, indeed, a "student work"—sometimes unpolished in its literary style and wandering or diffuse in its structure, but always overflowing with youthful enthusiasm and energy.

Included in this volume also are two versions of the life of Saint Aloysius. The first is from the Office of the saint, first published in 1737, and subsequently incorporated into the Roman Breviary. The other version (published in 1699) is somewhat longer and offers further beautiful details of his sanctity, piety, and ardent charity. A chapter from a third life of the saint, entitled *Speculum Innocentiae* (*The Mirror of Innocence*), is also provided, in which various wondrous instances of the actions of the angels in preserving the life of Aloysius are described.

It is interesting and illuminating to note that the personal spiritual mentors of Aloysius included both Saint Robert Bellarmine and Saint Charles Borromeo. The former acted as his confessor and spiritual director and, following his death, was an enthusiastic witness to his protégé's precocious sanctity and a committed campaigner for his beatification. The latter prepared him for his first reception of the Holy Eucharist. In later years, he was to make the life of Aloysius required reading for all nuns and virgins living within his own diocese of Milan.

In 1739, Pope Clement XII granted a plenary indulgence to all persons undertaking some act of piety or veneration towards Aloysius for six consecutive

Sundays. The decrees establishing these are given here, as well as a set of six weekly meditations, published in 1744 as a means of providing a fruitful way of fulfilling the requirements of the plenary indulgence.

Saint Aloysius, as patron of youth and students, has already guided and inspired countless thousands of young people by the example of his innocence of life and by his fervent and self-giving charity. It is hoped that his principal literary testament, the *Meditations on the Holy Angels*, may equally serve to promote the love of God, the veneration of the angels, and the desire for the life of heaven amongst contemporary readers.

> *Sancti Angeli custodes, defendite nos!*
> *Sancte Aloysi, ora pro nobis!*

> Fr. Robert Nixon, OSB
> *Abbey of the Most Holy Trinity,*
> *New Norcia, Western Australia*

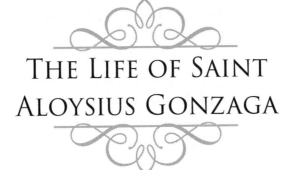

THE LIFE OF SAINT ALOYSIUS GONZAGA

From the Officium in Festo S. Aloysii Gonzagae (1737)

ALOYSIUS, THE SON of Ferdinand Gonzaga, Marquis of Castiglione delle Stiviere,[1] was in imminent peril of death from his very infancy, and for this reason, he was baptized with the greatest urgency and promptitude. Thus it was that almost before he had been fully born into this world, he was born into the life of heaven through the outpouring of sacramental grace.

This baptismal grace he retained with perfect constancy and faith, as one in whom divine sanctification has been unshakably confirmed. When he was but nine years old, he made a vow of perpetual virginity before

---

[1] Located in the Lombardy region of northern Italy.

an altar of the Blessed Virgin in Florence. From that time onwards, he always considered the Mother of God to be his very own mother.

By the grace of God, he was liberated and protected from all attacks of temptation, either in the flesh or in the mind. Nevertheless, he experienced all the typical distractions of youth but fought against these valiantly. He disciplined himself to control his physical senses so much that he would barely permit himself to look at the face of any female, even his own mother. Thus he came to be referred to as a "human who has transcended the flesh" and to be seen by many as an angel in human form.

He would fast on bread and water for three days every week and frequently kept vigils of prayer throughout the night. Often, he would remain completely still, positioned upon his knees, for three, four, or even five hours, while his soul was taken up in divine contemplation.

After a bitter dispute of three years' duration with his father—who strongly objected to him entering religious life—he joined the Society of Jesus. Although he was heir to vast wealth and the most exalted titles of nobility, he gladly handed all of these over to his younger brother. And even while he was a novice in the

Jesuit order, he exhibited himself to be a true master of all the virtues.

His love for God was so ardent that he often seemed to leave his body behind in flights of mystical ecstasy. Driven by fervent charity, he gave himself to the service of public hospitals and hospices for victims of the plague, which had flared up aggressively in Rome at that time. In the course of this ministry, he himself was infected by the dreaded disease.

After slowly being consumed by the torments of this virulent malady, his soul departed from this earthly realm to enter the kingdom of heaven on the twenty-first day of June, a date which he had already predicted. He was then only twenty-three years of age. In a vision, God permitted Saint Mary Magdalene de Pazzi[2] to see Aloysius in paradise enjoying all the glory of celestial beatitude. As a result of what she saw in this revelation, she declared the saint to enjoy the status of a martyr in heaven for his self-sacrificing charity and sanctity, although he was not officially known as such.

After the death of Aloysius, many remarkable miracles were obtained through his intercession. Pope

---

[2] A Carmelite nun and mystic (1566–1607) who was canonized in 1699.

Benedict XIII canonized him,[3] proposing him as a wonderful model and exemplar of innocence and chastity for all young people and declaring him to be the patron saint of youth and students.

---

[3] Aloysius was canonized in 1726. He had been beatified in 1605, only fourteen years after his death, by Pope Paul V.

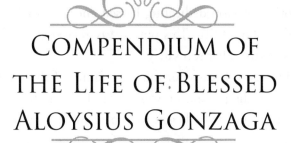

COMPENDIUM OF THE LIFE OF·BLESSED ALOYSIUS GONZAGA

By Jacob Bidermann (1699)

BLESSED ALOYSIUS WAS begotten of most illustrious parents, his father being Ferdinand Gonzaga, a Prince of the Holy Roman Empire and the Marquis of Castiglione delle Stiviere, while his mother was Martha Tania, a beautiful and holy woman of royal blood.[1] He was born in Castiglione delle Stiviere and first beheld the light of day on March 9, 1568. His mother was in grave peril as his birth approached, and the physicians

---

[1] His mother's family line had also included two popes, Sixtus IV and Julius II.

all despaired of the life of both the mother and her infant. As a consequence, she made a pious vow to the Mother of God dedicating herself and her son to her if they should live. This prayer was answered, and she gave birth to her son safely.

However, because of the uncertainty of the infant's survival, the precaution was taken of having him baptized as soon as he began to appear from his mother's womb. Thus it was that even before Aloysius had been fully born into this world, he was reborn in grace into the life of heaven through the sacramental waters of holy Baptism. Truly this was a rare privilege that God willed to initiate him as His own even before he had gone forth from the womb!

This special grace was fulfilled in the piety which Aloysius exhibited even as a child. For when he was but seven years old, his greatest intention was to honor God, the holy angels, and the saints. Each day, he would devoutly venerate these upon his knees, reciting the Office of Our Lady, the penitential psalms, and various other prayers. Never did he permit a single day to pass by without completing these devotions, even when he was gravely afflicted with illness. Indeed, this was a frequent experience for him as his physical constitution was frail. As a child, he once suffered from quatrain fever for a period of no less than eighteen months.

Inflamed by a fervent desire to please the great Mother of God, at the age of nine, he vowed himself to perpetual virginity before an altar dedicated to the Blessed Virgin in Florence. This vow he always preserved with complete perfection, both in a physical and spiritual sense. He received a very rare gift from heaven: that never once was he afflicted or troubled by any improper lusts or desires of the flesh, and neither was his mind ever stained by any illicit impulses or drawn to any forbidden delights or sinful pleasures.

He studiously avoided private contact with women, even those of the most illustrious and respectable rank and those related to him by blood. In fact, he even preferred that chaperones were present when he met with his own mother.[2] On account of his single-minded devotion and complete freedom from the temptations of the flesh and the world, he came to be referred to by many as "an angel who has descended from heaven."

---

[2]　This practice seems to have sprung from the concern of Aloysius that even legitimate familial ties should not distract him from God but rather should be governed by a certain degree of reserve. It does not reflect contemporary attitudes of the Catholic Church.

When he resided in the splendor of the palace of his father, there was one particular pleasure for him—namely, the frequent reception of the sacraments of the Holy Eucharist and Reconciliation. He engaged in the most ardent discourses and discussions on matters relating to divine and heavenly things and customarily lost himself in profound and ecstatic contemplation for many hours of the day and night. He avoided entertainments and games, even those of the most respectable kind.

Throughout his life, Aloysius exhibited the most obedient reverence towards his superiors and seniors, as well as humility amongst his peers. He deliberately neglected external splendor and luxury and preferred to wear old and simple garments. His custody of his eyes[3] was chaste and assiduous. Above all, he strove always to make his actions conform perfectly with the will of God. So faultless, exact, and immaculate was he in his observance of his religious life that he seemed to be a pure spirit, or a being without flesh.

In order that he would sleep more lightly and so be ready to waken for prayers at any time of the night, it

---

[3] The term "custody of the eyes" refers to control of what one looks at and the avoidance of looking too attentively at distracting or curious sights and, in particular, at attractive persons of the opposite sex.

was his custom to scatter sawdust amongst his bedding. From the eleventh year of his life, he practiced great restraint at the table, avoiding delicacies and feasts but choosing the simplest food in order to sustain the needs of his body. Often, he would content himself with a single boiled egg as a meal.

While cultivating these and all other Christian virtues and after careful deliberation and discernment, he resolved to renounce his exalted privileges and status in the world and to enter the Society of Jesus. There was one particular incident which especially confirmed him in this decision. Once, on the feast of the Assumption of the Blessed Virgin, after having received the Blessed Sacrament, Aloysius was kneeling in prayer before an icon of Our Lady. And—behold!—he heard the image speak to him the following words, "Enter the Society of Jesus!" This miraculous incident caused that particular icon to be given the title "Our Lady of Good Counsel," and it is venerated with deep devotion to this very day, especially in Madrid.[4]

---

[4] There are some divergences in various versions of the history of this particular icon. At the time when this life was written (1699), there was an Imperial Jesuit College in Madrid with a chapel dedicated to Our Lady of Good Counsel with an image of St. Aloysius kneeling before her. This icon clearly reflects the tradition recorded here.

Following the decision of Aloysius to join the Jesuits, he was to struggle for some three years before he was able to join. For, indeed, there were many within his own household and family who wished to prevent him entering the order.[5] But finally, after firmly persisting in his intention in the face of such objections and adversities, and having obtained the permission of his parents, he entered the novitiate of the Jesuits in Rome on April 2, 1582. Before joining the order, he formally transferred all his prerogatives and hereditary expectations to his younger brother. According to one reliable witness, the joy which Aloysius felt at renouncing these worldly treasures and honors exceeded that which his brother felt in receiving them.

When he was led to the cell where he would be accommodated for the initial period of his formation with the Jesuits, he exulted with all of his soul,

---

[5] This is presumably because, as the heir to a significant estate and important noble rank, it would have been seen as unbecoming for Aloysius to renounce these and enter religious life. It seems also possible that some of his family members or relatives may have felt that the austerities of religious life would have had a bad effect on the health and well-being of Aloysius, who (as has been noted) was of a frail physical constitution. Furthermore, Aloysius was only eleven years old when he formed his intention of entering the Jesuits, and such an early entrance into religious life (even as a scholar) may have seemed injudicious.

exclaiming the words of the psalm, "This shall be my place of repose throughout this age: here shall I inhabit, for I have chosen it for myself!"[6]

One particular virtue which shone forth radiantly amongst the many he possessed was that of the most exact observance of all rules. This he embraced with the greatest ardor and commitment. Indeed, before his death, he honestly confided to the rector at the College of Rome that never once had he deliberately infringed any of the rules or regulations of the order in even the smallest matter.

When he entered into higher studies of philosophy and theology, he continued with unbroken constancy in his prayer and meditation. All his academic efforts were made not for his own glory or credit but solely with a view to contributing to the glory of God and the Church. Although his instructors esteemed his intelligence and abilities as far exceeding those of any of his peers, he always retained the most sincere humility. He undertook his scholastic work with an unvarying intention of prayer and with a perfectly composed and attentive mind.

---

[6]   Psalm 131:14.

Aloysius continued to be blessed with the grace of contemplation during this time, as his own words demonstrate. Often, as he related, he would experience his spirit to be raised up and wander in celestial contemplation for a period of what seemed like six months when, in reality, only the duration of a single *Hail Mary* had elapsed. His love for the Eucharist was so great that he would spend three days in spiritual preparation before receiving the sacrament and spend the three days which followed in giving thanks to God.[7]

As long as he lived, he had an enthusiastic zeal for winning souls for God. Yet it is to be believed that God chose him, on account of his ardent virtue and angelic sanctity, to serve as a special and hallowed sacrifice of charity and to join the choir of the blessed with all promptitude—and therefore, through the action of the Holy Spirit, hastened his departure from this earthly sphere.

At that time, a fierce and deadly plague afflicted the people of Rome, and many members of the Society of Jesus were also suffering from this disease. Aloysius sincerely begged of his superiors that they grant him permission to serve the brethren who were ill.[8] Seeing his

---

[7]   At this stage, daily reception of the Blessed Sacrament, even for religious, was not the usual practice.

[8]   This seems to imply that he was engaged in serving in a hospital for Jesuits who were ill, whereas the previous life

fervor and the spirit of charity which animated him, he entered into this service of love with the utmost devotion, patience, and tenderness. Such was his compassion and diligence that he nursed even those whom the ravages and foulness of the disease had rendered most repulsive to the senses.

Not surprisingly, the plague soon took hold of Aloysius himself. On the seventh day of his infection, when death appeared to be nigh, he requested the last rites and the sacraments of the dying. These he duly received. But at that point, the disease suddenly transformed itself into a violent fever characterized by wide swings of temperature, from icy chills to burning sweats. He was to suffer from the grave pains of this affliction for a further three months. Yet all the while he was filled with surpassing joy and serenity, for he had often experienced a desire for martyrdom, which he felt was now being fulfilled.

He filled this time with piety and prayer towards God, the Blessed Virgin, and the holy angels, and in contemplation of the joys of the celestial paradise. Even in his illness, he would cast himself to the ground and

---

indicates it was a plague-hospital for the public. Given the strict regulations governing religious life at the time (particularly for juniors), it is much more likely that Aloysius was permitted to work in a hospital for sick religious rather than a public hospital.

recite the seven penitential psalms and other prayers and devotions. Thus he continued to accumulate a great treasure of merit for himself until his very last day.

He had long predicted that his death would occur on the octave day of Pentecost.[9] When this day arrived, he received once again the holy viaticum.[10] Invoking the most noble name of Jesus and with the most tender outpourings of affection towards the crucified Savior, he returned his soul to his Creator. This soul was, to be sure, completely free from the stain of sin and untainted by the lethal venom of earthly desires. Aloysius died on June 21, 1591.

Now, on the night before he died, he was absorbed into a continuous mystical ecstasy. As he saw the priest enter his cell in order to administer to him the last rites of the viaticum, he exclaimed, "With joy we depart! With joy we depart!"

Soon after his passing from this world, Saint Mary Magdalene de Pazzi received a mystical vision in which she saw Saint Aloysius exulting amongst the citizens

[9]   This means the eighth day after the solemnity of Pentecost, which was celebrated with a particular liturgical observance at the time.

[10]   The viaticum is the reception of the Eucharist by a person before impending death in order to assist his soul on its journey to the next life.

of heaven. Perceiving the celestial splendor by which his angelic soul was enveloped, she wrote of him thus: "O, how immense is the glory that has been given to Aloysius, the son of Ignatius![11] I never would have credited the magnitude of the glory and beatitude he has attained, had my Jesus not revealed it to me."

Both during his lifetime and after his death, the sanctity of Aloysius was demonstrated by a multitude of miracles. Indeed, no less than 206 miracles connected with him were considered and accepted by the Roman curia in the process of his canonization.

During the time when Aloysius was struggling in the throes of his impending death, his own father, the Marquis of Castiglione delle Stiviere—who had earlier strongly opposed his entrance into the Jesuits— underwent a deep religious conversion brought on by witnessing his dying son's sanctity and courage. He declared, "It is Aloysius who has obtained for my heart these salubrious pangs of sorrow and compunction whereby my own soul shall be saved!"

Pope Clement VIII, in conversation with the Marquis following the death of his son, lamented deeply and with the most tender tears the passing of this holy

---

[11] Saint Ignatius Loyola, the founder of the Jesuits.

youth. He said, "This is one who served quietly and unostentatiously, and brought the grace of peace to his religious family. O blessed Aloysius, you now possess the rewards of your faith in heaven, free from all the afflictions and suffering of this passing world!"

In the year 1605, he was beatified by Pope Paul V. In 1621, Pope Gregory XV dedicated a magnificent altar to the memory of this saint with the utmost solemnity and veneration.

THE DEVOTION OF SAINT ALOYSIUS TO HIS GUARDIAN ANGEL

From Speculum Innocentiae: sive Vita Angelici Juvenis B. Aloysii Gonzagae (The Mirror of Innocence: or the Life of the Angelic Youth, Aloysius Gonzaga) by Babriel Hevenesis (1717)

THE TENDER AFFECTION which Aloysius possessed for his guardian angel constantly increased as the holy youth advanced in age and maturity. Three times each and every day, he would devoutly commend himself to the protection of his guardian angel. Inspired by a desire to promote the love of, and devotion towards, one's guardian angel, he once wrote, "Be certain that you have in your guardian angel a trustworthy leader, whom it behooves you to follow! Let whoever is blind, whoever is uncertain of their journey and its peril similarly trust in their angel with confidence and faith, for it is the providence of almighty God which assigns and directs this angelic protector." Once Aloysius had entered adolescence, he wrote a beautiful set of meditations upon these angelic spirits, which were published and merited much warm praise and sincere approbation.[1]

Never are these celestial guardians venerated in vain, and they always respond favorably to the piety exhibited towards them! For the angel who protected the saintly Aloysius never permitted his care nor his love to be lacking, even for a moment. This spiritual being returned many benefits to the youth for the veneration and piety which he nurtured towards him and spared him from many of the perils and hazards of this mortal life, as his own special protégé. It will be edifying to consider a few particular instances of this.

His father, the Marquis of Castiglione delle Stiviere, was a most heroic and courageous soldier. Bravely fighting for his most Catholic monarch,[2] he had earned

---

[1]   The work referred to here is the *Meditations on the Holy Angels*, published in this present volume.

[2]   The "most Catholic monarch" referred to here is King Philipp II of Spain, who was also king of Portugal and ruler of the

for himself great honor and renown by his outstanding deeds at arms. And just as many parents desire their offspring to follow in their own footsteps, so he wished to impart to young Aloysius the same military skills which he possessed so abundantly. Accordingly, before the boy had reached the age of four, he taught him to use miniature cannons, swords, and many other weapons specially made for the use of one of his small size. Not long after this, he took his young son into a real battle, having carefully clad him in a little suit of armor. He then commanded Aloysius, holding aloft a flag tied to a small lance, to lead the troops as they marched forth.

At this time, the future saint did not fully understand what was taking place. Naturally enough, it all seemed to him like a piece of exciting playacting, and he took great pleasure in his role. But then the enemy suddenly fell upon them, and he soon realized that it was not playacting at all but that his life was in real peril. As Aloysius fired his own small musket to defend himself and ward off the foe, the burning gunpowder

---

Kingdoms of Naples and Sicily and of various other European principalities. He was a devout Catholic who fought strenuously to defend Catholic Europe against the Ottoman invaders and Protestant forces.

and scorching heat which were released wounded his delicate face.

In the chaos which surrounded him, he was entirely destitute of any human help. Pushed to and fro by the battle and the force of the discharging cannons, he fell backwards onto the ground. And as he did so, the wheel of a heavy carriage drew near where his head lay. His skull would certainly have been crushed, but—lo!—just at that moment, his guardian angel stopped the rushing wheel and saved the life of the pious boy from what was otherwise certain death.

O my reader, consider how many times in this life perils would have overcome you had your guardian angel not solicitously turned them away! Indeed, since you have survived to this day, it is certain that your guardian angel has done this already a vast multitude of times, the majority of which are wholly unknown to you. For each time you take a step on a slippery pavement, or mount a horse, or draw water from a well, you could very easily fall to your death by a single wrong step. And there are thousands of other instances in which death could easily befall you—by diseases, disasters, accidents, and misfortunes of every kind—unless your guardian angel were constantly protecting you.

And do you, for your part, offer this guardian angel of yours any reciprocal love or commensurate gratitude? This angel is constantly vigilant, both day and night, lest you should fall into any harm. Does it not therefore deserve at least one act of gratitude or veneration from you at least once a day? After all, you pay your servants their due wages, and you express polite appreciation for any gifts or services you receive. But what recompense do you offer your guardian angel, who serves you more constantly and faithfully than any human servant? O reader, make a resolution with yourself today to show gratitude to your spiritual protector, and adhere to this resolution assiduously! Count any day on which you fail to offer thanks to your guardian angel to be a "lost day." For you are always in need of the protection of this heavenly being, just as Saint Aloysius was always in need of his own.

Another instance of this occurred one day when Aloysius was crossing the Ticino River in his home region, riding upon a small horse-drawn carriage. Now at the time, it had been raining heavily, and the river was swollen and turbulent. As Aloysius passed over a flooded ford in the river, suddenly the force of the water swept his carriage away, taking him with it! It seemed almost certain that the life of the hapless youth would be lost in the swirling waves of the furious river. But, through the intervention of his guardian angel, the carriage was caught upon the trunk of a great tree, where it was held secure. Thus the boy was able to escape being submerged in the waters and to wait there unharmed until rescuers arrived and returned him to the welcome safety of the dry land.

On that occasion, it was water which menaced the life of Aloysius, but at another time, it was fire. For once he was afflicted with an illness and lay resting in his bed at night. Then it suddenly occurred to him that he had not yet said his daily prayers. So at once he called for a servant and ordered him to bring a lighted candle. He directed him to place the candle, in its stand, on his bed and then dismissed him. With his prayer book in hand, Aloysius was thus able to read his daily prayers, psalms, and meditations. Yet as he did so, he grew weary and fatigued, and sleep overtook him. But the lighted candle continued to burn down steadily until the bed sheets caught fire!

The voracious flames quickly enveloped these. And Aloysius, too, would certainly have been incinerated were it not for the timely intervention of his guardian angel. For this angel roused him from slumber just in time to flee from his burning bed, and so he escaped from the ravenous fire—his young life saved once more by his heavenly protector.

Following the incidents related here, it was only natural that Aloysius should be inspired with a most fervent gratitude and devotion towards the holy angels, and in particular towards the spiritual entity who served him as his own special guardian and protector. And, recognizing the Lord who created and commands these celestial beings, he endeavored always to do what was in conformity with the will of God, both in dealing with his own business and that of his father.

And the hope he placed in God was not deceived or frustrated, for it is said of Aloysius that there was never anything which he requested in prayer—either small or great—which he did not obtain, and there was no business, however difficult or apparently desperate, which he commended to the Lord which did not come to pass precisely as he wished.

May our own trust in God be like that of Saint Aloysius! Let us place our hope and confidence in Him alone and not in the vain things of this world. For, truly, the one who places their hope in the things of this passing world—which all soon vanish as fleeting shadows—builds his house upon sand and wavers like a feeble reed in the wind. But, O reader, make God, together with the angels who serve Him, your protector and your help, and all shall surely go well for you!

Do you wish God to be merciful and generous towards you? You can do this very easily: for God is the protector of all those who sincerely cultivate innocence of heart. Truly, an unstained conscience is the best refuge of the soul in any peril, for it alone unfailingly secures the invincible protection and assistance of the high King of heaven, together with His whole host of holy angels!

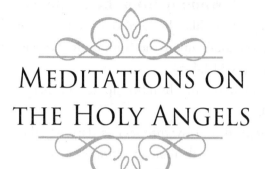

MEDITATIONS ON THE HOLY ANGELS

By Saint Aloysius Gonzaga

Testimony from the Gospel

"THE DISCIPLES APPROACHED Jesus, asking him, 'Who will be the greatest in the kingdom of heaven?'

"And Jesus called a little child to himself, and stood him in their midst. And he said, 'I tell you solemnly, unless you are converted and become like one of these little ones, you shall not enter the kingdom of heaven. But whoever humbles himself, like this little child, shall be great in the kingdom of heaven.

"'Take care that you do not disdain one of these little ones! For I tell you that their angels are always before the face of the heavenly Father'" (Mt 18:1–4, 10).

Testimony from the Prophets

"Who is there like the Lord our God, who dwells on high, yet looks upon the humble in heaven and on earth?" (Ps 112:4–5).

"God raises the humble up to the heights" (Job 5:11).

"I looked, and saw thrones raised up, and the Ancient of Days seated thereon in glorious majesty. And his raiment was radiant like snow, and his hair was like gleaming wool. And a thousand thousands ministered to him, and ten thousand times a hundred thousand attended him" (Dn 7:9–10).

"He has commanded his angels to protect you, that they guard you in all your ways" (Ps 90:11).

"He sent forth the angels of the Lord to all those who fear God, so that they may rescue them" (Ps 33:8).

"Do not say in the presence of the angels, 'There is no such thing as Providence!' For if you do so, God may be angered by your words, and destroy all the works of your hands" (Ecclus 5:5).

I. The Wondrous Grace of the Angels, and How It Is Fitting that the Church Venerates and Celebrates Them

Consider, esteemed reader, how Christ, for the sake of His great love for us, never ceases to bestow upon us new occasions for obtaining His grace and advancing in virtue. And He does this so that we may come to the ultimate goal which He has prepared for us—namely, everlasting happiness and perpetual peace. For this reason, Christ wills all the mysteries of our redemption to be devoutly celebrated so that the memory of these wonders may be constantly renewed in the minds of the faithful. Thus we recall all that the Lord suffered for the sake of our salvation, all that He did so that we should love and worship Him, and all the deeds of His holy life which He left us as an example to emulate.

But Christ was not content merely with this. For He left us also the wonderful memory of His most holy and blessed mother and of the entire communion of saints. He has created, too, the magnificent celestial hierarchy of the holy angels, those wonderful beings of radiant goodness and power. These serve faithfully as our protectors and patrons. They assiduously help us in all our needs, both spiritual and temporal. Furthermore, they furnish us with a multitude of edifying examples of sanctity, fidelity, humility, and virtue to meditate upon to the glory of God.

Since each one of us and the Church as a whole have received so many benefits from the holy angels, Christ willed that we should celebrate them also in solemn festivities and feasts. And certainly, since these holy angels desire and work so ardently to promote our salvation, it is only fitting that we should show to them our most abundant gratitude!

For this reason, Holy Mother Church observes diligently the feast of the glorious archangel Saint Michael, who is its singular and special protector.[1] It also celebrates a feast for all the other angels and archangels, indeed, for the whole celestial hierarchy.[2] For, as the Apostle testifies,[3] all of these angelic beings serve as helping spirits, working for the salvation of the souls of all the elect.

These glorious spiritual beings are constantly ready to go forth as assistants and helpers to humanity, despite the fact that they abide in a state far above our world of time and space. For they behold the glory of God and are inflamed with an ardent desire to serve Him. Knowing that it is God's will that human beings

---

[1]   September 29.

[2]   A feast for Holy Guardian Angels is observed on October 2.

[3]   See Hebrews 1:14.

be saved, for the sake of their love for God, the holy angels are prepared to go forth from the heavenly court and enter this earthly realm to provide assistance to human beings. Indeed, they are even ready to discard the magnificence of their spiritual forms and to assume the humble appearance of a corporeal human body in order to perform their duties more effectively. In such guises, the angels of the Lord sometimes enter into, and act within, our human society.

They do this so that they may help to build us up spiritually, from the wretched worms that we are, so that from the dust of our sin and weakness they may help fashion us into the towering walls of a heavenly Jerusalem and restore the chaotic ruins of our fallen humanity to the splendor of the image of God in which we were created. Indeed, these celestial beings bear a most profound and genuine love for all humankind for the sake of the overwhelming adoration they feel for the God who, through His glorious incarnation, came to partake fully in the condition of our humanity.

Consider also how apt is the Gospel reading used in the liturgy of the holy Church on the feast of the invincible archangel Saint Michael. For it is a passage which deals with the virtue of humility.[4] For, just as the haughty Lucifer was cast down from his throne in paradise to the depths of the inferno for his vain attempts to usurp the divine supremacy of God, so Saint Michael and the whole host of good angels were raised up to the highest honor and glory in the celestial court. Whereas Lucifer was cast down for his pride, Michael and the holy angels were exalted because of their humility in subjecting themselves to their Creator in adoration and obedience, and for their zeal for His glory. This Gospel is used, not only for the feast of Saint Michael, but also for the feast of All Holy Angels. All of these angels, together with the blessed Michael, attained to a crown of glory through the virtue of humility.

Through this, we human beings should understand that it is an ineffable, eternal, and divine decree that

---

[4] The Gospel passage referred to here is Matthew 18:1–4, 10, which, in the current lectionary, is given for the feast of the Holy Guardian Angels (October 2). "The disciples approached Jesus, asking him, 'Who will be the greatest in the kingdom of heaven?' And Jesus called a little child to himself, and stood him in their midst. And he said, 'I tell you solemnly, unless you are converted and become like one of these little ones, you shall not enter the kingdom of heaven. But whoever humbles himself, like this little child, shall be great in the kingdom of heaven. Take care that you do not disdain one of these little ones! For I tell you that their angels are always before the face of the heavenly Father.'"

no one shall ever arrive at the state of true and perfect glory, which the holy angels now possess, unless they follow the path of true humility. This path is beautifully demonstrated to us by the example of these holy angels, who subjected themselves fully to the will of God in love, obedience, and adoration.

Indeed, Christ our Savior Himself was glorified in His most sacred body through the virtue of holy humility. As the apostle Paul writes, "He humbled himself, and became obedient unto death, even death on a cross. Therefore God has highly exalted him, and given him a Name beyond all other names."[5] It is scarcely to be imagined that any of the faithful shall arrive at this same heavenly glory by any other path except that which was exemplified, taught, and sanctified by our head and master, Christ—namely, the lowly and gentle path of true humility.

II. The Excellence and Nobility of the Angels

Consider, O reader, the astounding and indescribable excellence of those noble princes of the celestial court of paradise! Of course, our mortal minds are not able to comprehend or imagine this fully. However, out of the

---

[5] Philippians 2:8.

small fraction of the brilliant light of the angels which we do perceive through their actions and presence, we may strive to glimpse something of the splendor of God's radiant and ineffable glory, which is reflected so magnificently in the holy angels.

There are three elements which serve to make a royal court illustrious, or to make an army great and admirable. The first of these elements is the nobility of the persons who form it. The second is the magnitude and number of its members. The third is the harmonious and beautiful ordering of its ranks and constituents. In each of these three elements, the heavenly court of the angels is found to be altogether marvelous and faultlessly perfect!

With regard to the nobility of the angels, we need only consider that they possess a privileged place amongst all the creations of God. For they are of a purely spiritual substance and of an immortal nature, immune from the sufferings, disease, aging, and death to which corporeal beings are all subject. Their intelligence is such that they are free from all errors and ignorance with respect to knowledge of created things. In addition to this perfectly illuminated light of intelligence, the angels possess a will which is completely and utterly constant, such that it may not be overcome or made to waver by any perturbation or adversity.

Regarding the blessed state of the holy angels, since they are entirely free from sin, they enjoy glory and eternal happiness without impairment. Moreover, they are richly adorned by the gifts of divine grace and therefore rendered most beautiful and pleasing in the sight of God. In their faculties of understanding and perception, they are enlightened directly by the radiance of celestial glory and are therefore rendered capable of seeing their Creator face to face. And in the will of the holy angels, charity is unimpaired by any sin, vice, weakness, or error. Thus they love God with a perfect and pure love and become like intimate friends or beloved children of His.

O my soul, contemplate the surpassing beauty of these citizens of paradise! They shine like a vast constellation of radiant stars, or even like the sun itself, in the splendid city of God. They are like a multitude of gleaming, polished mirrors of the divine perfection. In these brilliant mirrors, the infinite power, the eternal wisdom, the ineffable goodness, and the burning love of the Creator are most faithfully reflected.

O, how loveable, how pure and radiant are these blessed, angelic spirits! How zealous they are in defending the glory of God, and how solicitous and assiduous they are for the salvation of humans! It is therefore most fitting that we should love them and honor them with special devotion. Indeed, the philosophers define "honor" as being the reverence due to anyone on account of their virtue or excellence. It is for this reason that we show particular honor to human beings who surpass others in some praiseworthy characteristic, despite the fact that human beings are, in their essential nature, all equal. But the angels, even the very least of them, far exceed any mortal creature in their essential being and nature. How greatly, therefore, we should honor them!

Moreover, the angels, who are so noble and highly exalted both by nature and grace, humbly show unceasing love, honor, and solicitude in the service of human beings. How fitting it is that we should sincerely reciprocate this love and devotion! The angels love human beings because God Himself loves human beings. And human beings should love and honor the angels because God Himself loves and honors the angels.

For they are like dear children to God, who always lovingly contemplate His face as that of an honored Father. The angels are the glowing and spotless lilies amongst which the Deity grazes.[6] They are the lofty mountains filled with fragrant perfumes in which the

---

[6]   See Song of Songs 2:16.

heavenly Spouse joyously wanders; the verdant hills in which the divine Son takes His recreation![7]

III. The Vastness of the Multitude of the Angelic Host

Having considered the excellence and dignity of the angels, we should now turn our attention to the multitude and order of these spiritual beings. Firstly, as regards to the number of the angels forming the heavenly host, they far exceed the total number of all human beings together. And this is not only the human beings who are now alive but all who have ever lived and all who will ever live, from the beginning of the world until the Day of Judgment. The multitude of these blessed spirits is comparable to the number of grains of sand in the sea, or the number of stars in the firmament, which the wisdom of Scripture tells us can never be counted. Saint Dionysius, in the ninth chapter of his *Celestial Hierarchy*, tells us that the number of angels in any one of their heavenly ranks surpasses the total number of material things of any kind in the entire universe![8]

---

[7]   See Song of Songs 2:8.

[8]   The *Celestial Hierarchy* is a work attributed to Pseudo-Dionysius (traditionally identified with Dionysius the Areopagite. See Acts 17:34). Originally written in Greek, it was widely

The prophet Daniel writes, "A thousand thousand ministered to him, and ten thousand times a hundred thousand attended him."[9] Here, according to the custom of Scripture, the prophet provides a definite number to represent an indefinite one. The numbers he provides are indeed the greatest that the human mind can grasp, and even then, only with immense difficulty. By this he shows that the number of angels, while comprehensible to God, is beyond the powers of the human mind to imagine. While not objectively infinite, the number of angels resembles infinity from a mortal perspective, being wholly beyond our capacity to count or envisage. For this reason, we read in the book of Job the rhetorical question: "Can the multitude of God's host be numbered?"[10] And the royal prophet, David, speaking of the number of the angels, writes, "The chariots of God are tens of thousands many times over, together with many thousands who are rejoicing; for the Lord is among them, in Sinai, in his holy place."[11]

---

available in Latin translations during the Renaissance. Saint Thomas Aquinas had treated it as an authoritative source, and it would have been standard reading for students of theology during the time of Saint Aloysius.

[9]   Daniel 7:10.

[10]   Job 25:3.

[11]   Psalm 67:18.

The holy Evangelist, Saint John, writing in the book of Revelation, describes his vision of an enormous multitude in the presence of God, of every people, tongue, and nation. And he says that this multitude is not able to be numbered.[12] Now if the number of the elect, which we know to be only a small portion of humanity, is not able to be numbered, how much more so must this be true of the holy angels, who exceed tenfold the total number of all human beings who ever lived?

It is but fitting that the Sovereign and Monarch of the heavens should have such an immeasurable number of servitors and attendants in His celestial court. The wisdom of Sacred Scripture tells us, "The dignity of a king is to be found in the multitude of his people; and in the fewness of his subjects, the ignominy of a prince."[13] Now, since God is the most peerlessly exalted, noble, and powerful of kings—indeed, the very King of kings and the Lord of lords—it is appropriate that He should have an uncountable number of beings who form His household and His court in the immense and spacious palace of the kingdom of heaven.

O my soul, how much joy and solace shall you know when you are permitted to perceive such a vast multitude

---

[12] See Revelation 7:9.
[13] Proverbs 14:9.

of beings who are all so noble, splendid, and gracious! How unspeakably wonderful if you attain to the blessed destiny of joining this celestial assembly! For they are like princes of heaven and children of God—and you shall be as a brother or a sister, and a peer among them!

Indeed, these angelic spirits, transcendent though they are, shall not be ashamed to accept human beings as their brothers and sisters. For their Lord and God did not disdain, not only to assume the guise of a mortal, but truly to become a human being and to dwell amongst us. Through His glorious incarnation, God willed to become the true brother of each and every human being. O reader, how joyfully you should unite your voice with those of the vast and glorious company of holy angels in blessing and extolling the Lord for the multitude and immensity of the benefits you have received from Him!

IV. The Harmonious and Glorious Order of the Celestial Hierarchy

Next, let us turn our attention to the marvelous ordering of the angelic spirits, both amongst themselves, and in relation to God, and towards other created beings. This wondrous ordering was determined and established by the wisdom and power of Divine Providence.

If one considers how the holy angels relate to God, they worship Him in perfect unity and harmony, as if with one heart and mind. This worship is of the most devout reverence and is given to God as their supreme monarch and unrivaled Lord of their heavenly homeland.

If one considers how the angels are ordered among themselves, there is not the slightest trace of confusion or uncertainty among them, despite the incomprehensible vastness of their number. Rather, there is the highest and most perfect order and the most admirable diversity without any discord. Although there is no hint of rivalry, one angel may be higher and more excellent than another. And this is in perfect accordance with the diverse ways God intends to employ them for the service of Himself and humankind.

The whole multitude of these most glorious spirits is divided into three principal hierarchies: supreme, middle, and lower. Each of these three hierarchies are, in turn, divided into three distinct choirs—namely, a higher choir, a middle choir, and a lower choir.

The first and most exalted of the hierarchies comprises the three uppermost choirs of angels: the Seraphim, the Cherubim, and the Thrones. The function of each of these ranks of angels may readily be known by their names—it is, indeed, characteristic of God's wisdom to assign names to things according to their purpose. The function of the first and highest choir, that of the Seraphim, is to serve as a kind of confidential, intimate court to the King of heaven. In a manner that befits their name, they are not only inflamed with ardent love for God but burn like a radiant, spiritual fire which enkindles and illuminates all the lower ranks.[14]

The next rank of angels are the Cherubim. These are called by this name on account of their plenitude of knowledge and the brilliance of their intelligence. In respect to knowledge and intelligence, they surpass all the lower ranks and perceive God more clearly and know Him more profoundly than any others, except for the Seraphim. Thus they serve as wise advisors and trusted counselors to the celestial King, ennobled with all wisdom and intelligence. And the Cherubim communicate this wisdom and intelligence, which they possess so abundantly, to all the lower ranks of angels.

---

[14] The word "Seraph" means "burning one" in Hebrew. It is, of course, extremely unlikely that Saint Aloysius studied Hebrew to any great extent. Rather, his knowledge of the meaning of this word, together with the meaning of "Cherubim" (and the arrangement and functions of the angelic ranks in general) seems to be derived from *The Celestial Hierarchy* of Pseudo-Dionysius, to which Aloysius has referred previously.

Next, think of the choir of Thrones. These are like familiar friends and helpers to God. They are adorned with their particular name, for they are like seats or thrones of the divine Majesty in which He may comfortably repose and rest. Moreover, wherever these Thrones travel or are sent, they bear with them something of the presence of God.

If we now proceed to the middle hierarchy of angels, there are three choirs—namely, the Dominations, Virtues, and Powers. Each of these ranks are assigned to the governance of the ranks which are lower than themselves. The Dominations exercise their power like regional governors or ambassadors of the supreme Prince, working according to the mysteries of the divine will. Next, the Virtues share in something of the infinite virtue and strength of their Lord to perform difficult and arduous tasks on behalf of God within the realm He created, producing miraculous effects for the glory of their King. The third choir of angels in this middle hierarchy are the Powers. These exercise the power and authority of their Master, who is the highest Judge. They work industriously to remove all obstacles and impediments which may prevent human souls from entering into salvation.

If we move then to the third and lowest hierarchy of the celestial court, we encounter then the three final choirs of angels. These are the Principalities, Archangels, and Angels. The Principalities are called by this name because it is their role to fulfill the commandments and orders of the supreme Prince—God—whom they represent. Each one is assigned a particular region or province of the earth to oversee and superintend. These Principalities receive the orders of God, which they then communicate to the lower choirs—that is, the Archangels and Angels. These final two choirs of angels, the Archangels and Angels, are the ones who deal directly with human beings and the created world, acting as emissaries of the King of heaven. They are also the ones who are assigned to particular human beings to act as guardians, guides, and protectors. The Archangels are assigned to more important tasks and missions than the Angels; apart from this, there is no essential difference between these final two choirs.

But it must be noted that everything we have described above reflects but the smallest fraction and most basic structure of the wonderful ordering of the hierarchy of the heavenly court. For the architecture and order of the household of God is of such a marvelous complexity and miraculous immensity that the human mind cannot hope to begin to comprehend it fully. If we could examine each angelic being individually, we would find that each and every one exercises some particular and unique function in the celestial Jerusalem. Indeed, as we gaze at the firmament at night, we behold the innumerable multitude of stars and planets, all moving with precision according to a harmonious and divinely ordained plan. In just the same manner, God has ordered the multitude of His angels—whose incalculable number vastly exceeds that of the totality of the stars—in their respective roles and ministries. It is through these angels, like countless myriads of brilliant stars and planets rotating in their orbits, that God directs to human beings all the wonders of His graces, charisms, and loving protection.

V. A Prayer to the Angels

My soul, call to mind the queen of Sheba and the auspicious occasion on which she visited that most wise and prudent king, Solomon. She was so astonished with the stupendous number and admirable order of that great king's ministers and servants that (as Scripture says) she was quite overwhelmed.[15] This great

---

[15] 1 Kings 10:4.

queen declared to the wise Solomon, "Blessed are your ministers and blessed are your servants! For these have the privilege of standing in your presence and listening to your wonderful words of wisdom!"

O my soul, how much more reason do you have to be overwhelmed with admiration than did the queen of Sheba when she was astonished at the beauty and magnificence of the palace and household of the royal prophet Solomon! For if you contemplate the celestial court of the true Solomon—that is, of Jesus Christ, the King of kings and Lord of lords—you will perceive therein an immensity and order and a dignity which incomparably exceeds that of the earthly Solomon, or indeed the glory of any created thing, and even the whole visible universe itself. How much joy, rapture, and consolation shall you enjoy if, after the course of this mortal life, you are able to join the court of the heavenly King. For to serve this King, who is God Himself, is truly to reign forever!

O holy and pure angels, how truly blessed you are! For you stand perpetually in the presence of the Divinity, and with ineffable joy gaze forever on the beauteous face of the Monarch of the earth and skies, the Emperor of time and space. By the grace of this celestial Lord, you are adorned with supernal wisdom, enriched with unique privileges, and exalted to become worthy of the glory in which you partake and reflect.

O you radiant stars of the heavens, how splendidly you shine within the celestial firmament! Pour forth into my poor soul, I implore you, something of your blessed innocence and grace. Help me to preserve my faith without compromise or defect, and let my thoughts and deeds be free from the dark stain of guilt and earthly corruption. Help me ever to grow in love for God and for my neighbor!

I beseech you, O blessed angels of God, that by your protecting hands you guide me along the royal path of humility, which you yourselves so faithfully follow. When my earthly life is over, may I merit to contemplate the glory of the face of the eternal Father in your radiant company and be granted the privilege of occupying my very own place in the golden splendor of the celestial firmament as a star amongst the stars!

VI. Saint Michael, the Prince of the Heavenly Host

After our contemplation of the magnificence, beauty, and harmony of the angelic hierarchy as a whole, it is fitting that we now turn our attention to the invincible prince of the heavenly host, the archangel Michael. On account of his unwavering fidelity and burning zeal, he was established by God as a general or commander amongst the celestial armies. Indeed, he serves as a trusted leader to all the other angels, who perform the diversity of ministries assigned to them.

The name by which this most blessed spiritual being is honored, Michael, means "Who is like God?" For when Lucifer, impelled by pride and envy against God, wished to become like Him, this most powerful archangel, burning with ardent zeal and indignant at the offence given to the Most High, exclaimed, "Who is like God?" By this, he meant, "Who is so arrogant and bold that he should dare to compare himself to God?" By asking this rhetorical question, he expressed the manifest and holy truth that there is no created being, either in heaven or anywhere else in the entire universe, who can rival the one, supreme God.

O mighty and invincible Michael! You are truly worthy of the glorious name you bear. For you are blessed amongst all angels and worthy of all praise and honor from the human race! For it was you who were most zealous and faithful in vindicating and defending the glory of God against His foe.

This glorious angel has been enriched by God with countless privileges and honors, not only in the Church

Triumphant (in heaven), but also in the Church Militant (on earth). Under the covenant of the Old Law, he was appointed protector and guardian of the synagogue. And under the New Law—that is, the Gospel of Christ—he is exalted as defender and guide to the Church of God. This is the insuperable and awesome commander and captain whom the entire army of the heavens follows faithfully and loyally. Under his leadership and direction, the force of the good angels assembled and fought valiantly against the wicked temerity of the ancient serpent and attained a glorious victory over the enemy of God! And, led by Saint Michael, that radiant, celestial army cast the ancient serpent—that is, Satan—from the heavens, together with all his myriad minions of fiends and rebel angels.

Since the time of that primordial battle, Michael has always been prompt and ready at hand to raise himself for battle for the sake of the glory of God and the salvation of humankind. He is the one who fought for the people of God in Egypt when they were liberated from the yoke of Pharaoh's oppression by means of signs and wonders. He it was who struck down all the firstborn of the land of Egypt on that horrible night of death and slaughter which was the first Passover. He it was who for forty long years went before the tribes of Israel as they wandered through the desert wastes, acting as their ever-watchful guide and guardian. Through his power, the army of Pharaoh, who pursued the people of God, were submerged into the watery depths of the Red Sea. With his mighty arm and the blazing sword of sanctity, he laid to waste those people and nations who resisted the Israelites and eventually led them safely to the haven of the Promised Land.

After the death of Moses, when the cunning devil endeavored to draw the people of God away from the truths of sacred wisdom and to lead them into the darkness of idolatry, it was Michael who put the deceiver to flight. And as he performed all of these stupendous feats and heroic deeds, he was constantly inflamed by the most ardent zeal for the divine honor and for the salvation of the chosen people of God.

And after the people of Israel had been led into their exile in Babylon, it was Michael who led them forth once their ordained time of captivity had been completed. With a strong hand, he removed every obstacle to their freedom and opened the doors of liberty to them once more.

It is pertinent to note that although the name of Michael may not be expressly mentioned in the Scriptures in all of these events, nevertheless—since he was established as the particular protector and guardian to the people of Israel—one may believe with confidence that he, and perhaps other angels, were involved in carrying out these works in accordance with the will of God.

This most glorious archangel, apart from his role in providing general protection for the holy Church, has another special function—namely, that of receiving, protecting, and guiding the souls of the faithful after death as they make their journey from this world to the next. He will ward off the attacks of all malign demons and deliver the souls of the deceased safely to the tribunal of Christ, where they shall receive whatever recompense and reward is due to them according to their merits.

And then, when the end of this world arrives, Michael shall again appear as a mighty warrior and hero to engage in the final battle with the Antichrist,[16] who will endeavor to deceive the faithful by means of miracles and prodigies. This radiant archangel shall then valiantly protect the Church of God against the Antichrist and against the multitude of persecutions and foes who shall assail it. And once he has attained victory over the prince of darkness and cast him, bound, into the bottomless abyss of the inferno, then it is this

---

[16] See Revelation 12:13.

same archangel who shall blow upon the final trumpet. At the thunderous blast of this final trumpet, the dead shall arise from their graves[17] and be assembled before the eternal Judge—the just and righteous, to receive their blissful reward of eternal glory, while the wicked and sinners shall hear that dreaded sentence of unending damnation. Truly, indeed, at that stage, there shall be no further time or opportunity for mercy or for grace but only the most severe and exact justice of God. And according to this just and definitive judgment, each one shall go to their place of eternal habitation—heaven or hell—depending upon what they merited whilst in this world!

O invincible prince of the heavenly host and unfailing guardian of the Church and of the souls of the faithful! You have fought in so many fierce battles, inflamed with love and ardor. And each and every time you have fought, you have attained a glorious victory over the foe. This you have done not for the purpose of gaining personal fame or renown, as the generals and commanders of this world are accustomed to do. Rather you performed your deeds of heroism and valor purely to defend and protect the honor and glory of

---

[17] See 1 Thessalonians 4:16.

God and to promote and advance the salvation of the entire human race. In truth, this is something which all we Christians are bound to do also in our own way and in accordance with our state of life.

Come, O unconquerable Saint Michael, to the assistance of my soul! For it is continually attacked and assailed, assaulted and imperiled, by its enemies—namely, the flesh, the world, and the devil. Just as once you were mighty captain and leader to the people of Israel as they wandered through the arid wastelands of the desert, be unto me a faithful leader and companion as I make my way through the desert of this world. And may you finally lead my soul to the joyful land of the living, to that true heavenly homeland, for which all mortals on the earth deeply yearn as poor, banished exiles.

O my soul, when the dreaded hour of death arrives, filled with terror and struggle, you shall then be compelled to depart from the fragile tent of the mortal body, alone and naked, and to pass through the narrow portal of death! And then a fearsome multitude of infernal dragons and serpents, together with an army of the evil spirits of hell, shall surround you and grasp at you ravenously, like roaring lions seeking for whom they may devour.[18] At that terrifying moment of time, may this invincible archangel, Saint Michael, be prompt to come to your aid! May he fight on your behalf, guarding you with the unbreakable shield of his protection so that you may pass safely through the foes who surround you and arrive unharmed at your celestial homeland.

And, my soul, when you stand before the most exacting tribunal of final judgment, may this most glorious archangel stand beside you as your defender and advocate, answering for your conduct and imploring mercy on your behalf. Under the resplendent banner of his noble triumph, may he lead you to the most blessed light. There, he, together with all the holy angels and the souls of the elect, shines with ineffable and unending joy in the infinite glory of their Creator.

O my soul, if you have true confidence in the presence and assistance of Saint Michael, the prince of the heavenly host, you shall surely be ready to depart from this earthly realm with immense joy of heart and unwavering hope whenever the fateful hour of death arrives!

---

[18] See 1 Peter 5:8.

VII. Saint Gabriel, the Herald of the Incarnation and the Guardian of the Virgin Mary

Following our meditations upon the glorious Saint Michael, the prince of the heavenly host, it is fitting that we turn our attention now to Saint Gabriel and the dignity and exaltation of the prerogatives and virtues which he possesses. Although he is referred to in Scripture simply as an "angel,"[19] we should not imagine that he ranks merely among the lowest choir, who are given this particular designation. [For the term "angel" is used also to refer to the spiritual beings of any of the orders or ranks of the celestial court in a general sense, not the lowest rank only.] Gabriel certainly belongs to the higher choir of those spiritual beings who are sent to the assistance of humankind—namely, the archangels. Moreover, he has primacy amongst this magnificent and holy choir.

Just as the mysteries with which Gabriel was entrusted to communicate by God were of a special excellence and sublimity, so this legate of heaven is of a particular and distinguished nobility in the celestial hierarchy. He is the faithful and trusted friend of the spouse, to whom was revealed the awesome wonder of

---

[19] See Luke 1:26.

the divine Incarnation and the coming of the Word made flesh. And it was he who first revealed this saving mystery to the world. For he was chosen as the special mediator between the most high God and the humble Virgin of Nazareth, between the eternal Word and our human nature.

To understand and appreciate the outstanding dignity of this wonderful archangel, we may consider the importance of the mission assigned to him by God. Furthermore, we should bear in mind that—as many of the saints have noted and affirmed—Gabriel was appointed as a particular guardian to the Blessed Virgin herself. Now God created no other being more pure and more noble in all the heavens and in all the earth than the Virgin Mary. If you consider for a moment how princes in this world always entrust the treasures which are dearest to them to their most faithful and trusted servants, then you will be able to imagine how highly Gabriel is esteemed by God, since He chose to entrust to him His most dear and precious treasure— namely, His beloved spouse and mother, the blessed Virgin Mary.

Consider that it was this glorious archangel that was selected to act as the legate and spokesman for the Holy Trinity in attending to the most important matter which has ever occurred in this universe—that is, the incarnation of the only-begotten Son of God, and hence the redemption and salvation of the world!

For this reason, the name "Gabriel" is most suited to this archangel, for it means "the strength of God." For it was Gabriel who announced the most strong and unbreakable bond established by the Incarnation—the mystical bond whereby God was united indivisibly and completely with our human nature. Since the divine nature was united with both a human body and soul in the person of Jesus, the Incarnation may be understood as the unbreakable "triple rope" referred to prophetically in Sacred Scripture when it is written, "A triple rope is not easily broken."[20]

Gabriel very rightly deserves the name "the strength of God" for another reason too. For it was the glorious outcome of his mission as a legate of God to the Blessed Virgin that something of the strength of God was communicated to, and bestowed upon, our human weakness and mortal frailty. Through the grace of the Incarnation, the Divinity was definitively united to our human nature, and human beings, as a consequence, came to share in something of the strength and power

---

[20] Ecclesiastes 4:12.

of the Godhead. Hence it is that through this strength of God, many of the saints—the apostles and martyrs—came to perform deeds and to endure sufferings in a manner which entirely exceeds the natural limits of human fortitude.

VIII. Saint Raphael and the Guardian Angels

Having considered the burning zeal and illustrious deeds of Saint Michael, the prince of the heavenly host, and the mystical strength and special privileges of the archangel Gabriel, it now remains to consider the diligent charity and solicitous love exhibited by the angel Raphael. By his own testimony, recorded in Sacred Scripture, he is one of the seven spirits who always stand in the presence of God.[21] From this fact, it is clear that his rank within the celestial hierarchy is a very exalted one indeed and that he is one of the very greatest of all the angels of paradise.

In the following discussion, we shall come to consider the many benefits which we each receive from our own particular guardian angel. For Raphael, by the offices of charity and protection which he exhibited to

---

[21] Tobit 12:15.

both Tobit and Tobias,[22] is shown to be a model of the benefits which our own guardian angels confer upon each one of us. In his actions, he typifies and illustrates the role assigned to each particular guardian angel.

The name "Raphael" signifies "the medicine of God." This appellation is most apt for this holy angel because of the spiritual and physical healing which his actions imparted to both Tobit and Tobias. It was by the divine medicine which Raphael administered that sight was restored to the afflicted Tobit and that Tobias was protected from the insidious assaults of a very wicked and murderous demon.

Please consider for a moment[23]—what is it that your own guardian angel does for you, except for providing you with divine medicine?

So that you may understand this more clearly, reflect upon the three different states of human life. The first

---

[22] In the Latin text, Aloysius uses the name "Tobias" for both the father and the son in accordance with the text given in the Vulgate. However, modern English translations use the name "Tobit" for the father and "Tobias" for the son. This nomenclature has been followed in the present translation to avoid confusion.

[23] There is a certain ambiguity here (perhaps intentional) as to whether Aloysius is addressing the reader or his own soul (i.e., that he is reflecting with himself in the manner of a soliloquy). This ambiguity has been intentionally retained in the translation.

state of life is that which takes place in the womb of one's mother from the moment of conception until the time of birth. The second state of life begins with the moment of birth and extends to earthly death, after which the particular judgment of the soul follows. The third state of human life is that which follows death. In each of these three states of life, you may reflect upon the benefits your guardian angel provides and find this to be congruent with the model shown in the actions of Saint Raphael.

In regard to the first state of life, Scripture narrates that when Tobit planned on sending his son, Tobias, to a distant region, he was solicitous to obtain for him a faithful companion for his travels. And—lo!—before this good youth had set a single foot out of his homeland, an angel sent by God—that is Raphael—appeared to him in human form. He offered himself as a companion and guardian to the young Tobias and promised to act as his guide for the whole of his journey.

O my reader, how immense is the love shown by our Creator to you! For even before you went forth from your mother's womb, before you encountered a single one of the perils of life and the snares of your foes, God had already given a command to one of his holy angels, one of the blessed spirits who eternally contemplate

His divine face. This guardian angel, appointed to protect you, had already began this task before you were born. While still being nourished within your mother's womb, and in a defenseless and vulnerable condition and subject to many possible perils, your guardian angel protected both you and your mother who carried you—and thus you were able to arrive safely and without impediment to the sacred grace of the baptismal font, and there to have your name inscribed amongst those of the children of God.

But now that you have reflected upon the care and love which God has shown to you while you were still growing in the womb of your mother, it is most wonderful to reflect that God—YHWH,[24] who perceives all time as a single instant—has been tenderly mindful of your safety and well-being for all eternity. He did this even before the foundations of the heavens and the earth were laid, before the angels were created, and before the primordial Chaos came into being. And, although God foresaw eternally that you would often fall into sin and frequently fail to show due gratitude to Him for His gifts, nevertheless He decreed—purely

---

[24] In the Latin text, Aloysius uses the name "Io" here, which was a transliteration of the divine name, the Tetragrammaton, used in Latin during the Renaissance.

out of His love and grace—not only to assist you in the course of this life from the very first moment of your conception until your death, but to lead you at last to the glorious bliss of eternal beatitude!

Turning now to the second state of human life—that is, after a person has come forth from the womb and entered the light of this earthly theater—Scripture tells us how the angel Raphael went forth with Tobias when he began his journey. [This is surely a figurative representation of a human being's commencement of the pilgrimage of mortal life.]

[Firstly],[25] Raphael promises Tobias that he will be a faithful companion to him for the entire course of his travels and will lead him safely to his true destination.[26] In the same way, from the very moment of your birth, you are accompanied by the angel—one of the citizens of the celestial city—appointed as your guardian by God. This angel receives you into his special protection

---

[25] In the text which follows, Aloysius lists six considerations of the actions of Raphael and one's own guardian angel. However, he numbers only the second and third of these points. The practice of enumerating points was a standard practice in theological writing at the time, and the omission of the numbering of the other considerations was almost certainly an oversight. They have been inserted into the present translation.

[26] See Tobit 5:5–21.

and patronage and acts towards you as a teacher and guide. Indeed, in this life, we are all like small children, constantly needing someone to act as our tutor and guardian. It is our guardian angel who does this, leading us by the hand and supporting us, lest the sharp rock of sin should pierce our foot or some sudden hazard overtake us. Often this guardian angel will take us up in his hands and tenderly carry us so that we are borne through some danger or peril before we are even aware of its existence.

Secondly, the angel Raphael provided the youth Tobias with wise counsel on his journey, instructing him concerning each of his significant actions. For example, he advised him to enter into marriage with Sarah and furnished him with instructions on how to overcome the demon who afflicted her by means of continence and prayer.[27] In the same manner, your own guardian angel provides you with good advice and directs your actions wisely in all things. It is this guardian angel who motivates and encourages you to perform good works, which—without his help and exhortation—you would surely not do. Sometimes, he does this by suggesting to you the holy example of Christ Our Lord. Other times,

---

[27] See Tobit 6:10–22.

he stirs up your will by consideration of, and gratitude for, the infinite benefits and blessings which God has so graciously bestowed upon you. And yet other times, your angel motivates you to doing good by calling to your mind the thought of the bliss of heaven and the torments of eternal damnation.

Thirdly, Scripture narrates the benefits which Tobias receives from Raphael with regard to his personal well-being and temporal necessities. For when Tobias arrived at the river Tigris and washed his feet in its waters, an immense fish leapt out to devour him. The angel defended him and freed him from this peril. Moreover, he instructed Tobias to seize the fish and to extract its gall to use as a medicine for restoring the sight of his blinded father, Tobit.[28] This same angel aided Tobias in obtaining the wealth and treasures which he had been sent forth by his father to recover.[29] But also—through his marriage to Sarah—he established him as heir to all the riches and vast estates of his father-in-law, Raguel.[30]

And, similarly, what do our own guardian angels do for us if not offer to us ready assistance in all our

---

[28] See Tobit 6:1–9.
[29] See Tobit 9:1–7.
[30] See Tobit 8:21–24.

own needs and trials? They keep their eyes upon us diligently and tirelessly, just like a loving mother who watches her child lest it should slip and fall or do anything foolish or dangerous. Consider how many physical perils your guardian angel has already protected you against! Reflect on how solicitous your guardian angel has been thus far in ensuring that you have had the temporal necessities for sustaining your life so that you have arrived at this day with your life and health intact. By means of this protection against physical dangers and the generous provision of temporal necessities, you have been given a privileged opportunity for attaining eternal salvation without impediment or distraction. How great is this blessing, how wonderful is this grace!

[Fourthly,] the angel Raphael performs the service of interceding and offering prayers to God for Tobias, as he himself testifies.[31] Similarly, your own guardian angel exercises the office of offering prayer on your behalf in the sight of God, acting as your advocate and procurator in heaven. By the intercession and agency of this angel, your prayers and desires are promptly conveyed to God, and this angel faithfully apprises God of whatever you do in the form of good works or acts

---

[31] See Tobit 12:12.

of piety. How wonderful it would be if we were able to see how industriously and untiringly our guardian angels ascend and descend from earth to heaven and from heaven to earth on our behalf, as if climbing the miraculous ladder perceived by the patriarch Jacob![32] In ascending, they communicate our needs to God through intercession and prayer on our behalf. In descending, they carry to us a multitude of gifts and graces from our heavenly Father: holy inspirations, good thoughts, and various other means of divine assistance and guidance. Furthermore, they also convey to us the paternal corrections of God from time to time so that we may become aware of our faults and be motivated to emendation and improvement lest we—together with this sinful world—should be condemned.

[Fifthly,] the angel Raphael instructed Tobias in the method he should use whereby he might conquer the demon [that had killed each of Sarah's previous suitors] so that it would have no power over him.[33] And this angel himself fought a courageous battle on behalf of the youth against this same maleficent spirit, soundly defeating him and casting him out into the desert.[34]

---

[32] See Genesis 28:10–17.
[33] See Tobit 6:14–22.
[34] See Tobit 8:3.

Thus does our own guardian angel do for each of us, like a trustworthy captain commissioned to defend a stronghold against its enemies. Our guardian angel remains alert and watchful lest any foes should capture and occupy the fort of our soul. These angels are the faithful guards whom the Lord has located on the walls of Jerusalem[35] to keep watch over His flock throughout the night lest the ferocious wolf of hell, who prowls around like a roaring lion seeking for someone to devour,[36] should seize upon our poor souls!

It is to these guardian angels that these words from the book of Revelation are addressed: "Be vigilant and strong."[37] For our guardian angel is ever vigilant against demons, repelling their incursions, breaking their powers, and repairing and restoring any injuries that we have received. He infuses strength to us by deterring us from sins and vices. For without the spiritual and practical assistance of such a guardian, we would surely slip easily into such pitfalls which surround us on every side. Our guardian angel does this sometimes by encouraging us and animating us to resist the temptation we encounter and to stand firm in the face of trials

---

[35] See Isaiah 62:6.
[36] See 1 Peter 5:8.
[37] Revelation 3:2.

and tribulations. At other times, he implores the Lord on our behalf so that, by divine grace, we are able to survive perils and to attain victory over our spiritual foes, even when our own strength and virtue would not otherwise suffice.

[Sixthly,] the angel Raphael defeated the demon who had killed all the previous men who had married Sarah.[38] He bound this demon up and drove him out into the desert.[39] This he did in order to save the life of Tobias and to ensure that he was happily and safely married to Sarah. In the same way, our own good angel will fight valiantly against all the foul demons who assail our souls. This is particularly so during the hour of our death. For it is at that time that we shall be attacked most bitterly and savagely by such hellish fiends, who prowl around like lions seeking one to devour.[40] This angel also defends the soul from attacks of despair and doubt—the sins which attack us during times of difficulty and adversity, and most especially when we arrive at the final moments of life. Thus, protected by our guardian angel, the soul may, at its moment of death,

---

[38] See Tobit 6:14.
[39] See Tobit 8:3.
[40] See 1 Peter 5:8.

escape from the miseries of the passing world and ascend to the unending joys of its heavenly homeland!

And when our soul has left the dwelling place of the body and stands before the awesome tribunal of divine judgment, our guardian angel will stand by its side as a faithful and effective advocate. And if it is necessary that the soul should expiate certain sins and be purified of vices in purgatory for a time after death, even there its guardian angel shall be its companion. It shall provide much-needed consolation and fortitude and inform the departed soul of all the prayers which are said for its attainment of eternal rest by those who remain on earth. Most importantly, it shall remind the soul under-going purgation and purification of the encouraging truth that now that it has entered purgatory, it is abso-lutely certain to reach heaven in due course.

Coming to the third and final stage of existence of the human soul—that is, after it has left this mortal life and entered the world beyond—consider how the angel Raphael, after he had united Tobias with Sarah as his wife, ensured that Tobias became the heir of all the treasures of his father-in-law, Raguel.[41] He also led Tobias, after the successful and profitable completion

---

[41] See Tobit 8:21–24.

of his long pilgrimage, back to his own beloved home-land and his father's house.[42] There, he was received with immense joy, proportionate to the sorrow at his departure and all the danger he encountered during his wanderings.

Contemplate now the services of your own guardian angel in relation to these events. For this angel will lead you back to your heavenly homeland after the long and perilous pilgrimage of this life is complete. Enriched with a multitude of gifts and graces, you shall be taken to the celestial paradise of eternal rest, which is your soul's true native land. You shall be led into the radiant splendor of the New Jerusalem! There, with outpour-ings of fervent joy and the exultation from the whole assembly of supernal spirits and blessed saints, your guardian angel shall happily present you. And there the hand of God Himself shall bestow upon you the golden crown of unfading glory and ineffable bliss, which has been prepared for you for all eternity. You will then have attained forever that splendid reward for which we all long and sigh throughout the trials and tribulations of this mortal life, as we mourn and weep here now as exiles in this earthly valley of tears.

---

[42] See Tobit 10–11.

O soul who has remained loyal to your Creator, you are a thousand times blessed! For after the completion of the assigned years of your mortal life, you shall be led into the star-adorned tabernacle of immortal beatitude. And there the glorious wedding banquet of the Lamb with *you*, His beloved spouse, shall be celebrated. There the plenitude of happiness, perfect peace, and rest shall be yours forever and ever!

IX. An Exhortation to the Soul

But, O my soul, throughout the entire course of your life thus far, you have frequently offended your Creator. You have caused much grief and anxiety to your guardian angel who has sought to preserve you in righteousness and virtue. However shall you dare to stand in the presence of the divine Majesty without shame and fear? Should you not rather despair of your salvation altogether?

Certainly not! For there is no limit or bounds to His divine mercy, and His forgiveness has no end. Like the good father who receives the prodigal son with the open arms of unconditional love, just so the Lord will welcome you. You have merely to long to return to your most merciful Father with genuine penitence for your sins and a genuine desire for His love.

What indeed are we able to repay to the Lord for such immense benefits and graces He has conferred upon us? For whatever we receive through the blessed spirits and saints and angels, we owe to the generosity and goodness of God Himself. For it is He who commands His angels to guard us in all our ways.[43] Oh, what fervent and sincere gratitude ought we to feel towards those blessed angels for the love and faithfulness towards us!

Above all, you should honor your guardian angel for his constant assistance. And you should never do anything in the sight of this angel which you would be ashamed to do before another human being. Alas for you if your guardian angel should find you unworthy of the care which he bestows upon you!

There are, however, many virtues which bring delight to these holy angels. They deeply desire to see these virtues flourish in our lives and in our hearts. Such things which please the angels include sobriety, chastity, voluntary poverty, and heartfelt prayers poured forth with tears and sighs. Above all these other virtues, though, they are delighted with peacefulness and fraternal charity. And our holy angels help us to attain all of

---

[43] See Psalm 90:11.

these virtues through their unceasing intercession and guidance.

O my soul, you are the most beautiful and lovely image of your Creator! How greatly are you loved by God, and how deeply esteemed you are by His angels! If you are ever mindful of not offending these glorious beings or causing them sorrow and distress, you shall then easily avoid the foul and vile stain of sin. For if there is such immense joy amongst the angels in heaven over the conversion of one sinner, how much sorrow must your own guardian angel feel whenever he sees you slip into sin and thus be separated from divine grace?

My soul, seek therefore to adorn yourself with all those virtues which exhilarate the angels and glorify the Creator! For, emulating the virtues of the angels, you shall surely come to enjoy the sweetest fruit of eternal bliss in their glorious company.

X. A Final Prayer

O Lord my God, you have assigned the services of the holy angels to humankind in a miraculous order and harmony. These are the same blessed spirits who stand in the presence of your divine Majesty in awe and reverence. Grant, O Lord, that my own life may be protected and guided by these blessed spirits and that I may be defended by their diligent care from the cruel attacks of my spiritual foes.[44]

O Lord, you have granted to your holy angels the fullest gifts of heavenly grace. Grant to me that through their prayers and intercessions, I may attain something of this grace by imitating their humility, charity, and purity in my own actions and thoughts.

May I strive to lead an angelic life even here on earth so that I may merit to share the company of the angels in heaven. Grant that, in due course, I may come to enjoy with them the most glorious vision of your divine splendor for all eternity! Amen.

---

[44] In the Latin text, this final prayer is written as if on behalf of another, in the second person. However, it seems as if this is Saint Aloysius speaking to his own soul, as has often occurred throughout the previous chapter. Accordingly, the English translation has been modified (substituting first-person forms for second-person forms) to convey its sense of being a personal prayer.

THE SIX SUNDAYS DEVOTION IN HONOR OF SAINT ALOYSIUS

Indulgence

I. Decree Concerning Indulgences Granted to Those Venerating Saint Aloysius Gonzaga for Six Consecutive Sundays

FATHER FRANZ RETZ, superior-general of the Society of Jesus, has graciously advised us of the custom adopted by many of making a special veneration of Saint Aloysius Gonzaga for six consecutive Sundays, either before the feast of the saint, or on other Sundays of the year. In response to the humble request of the aforementioned Father Retz, the Sacred Congregation for Indulgences and Holy Relics hereby grants—for the purpose of the promotion of divine worship and the advancement of the spiritual life of the faithful—a plenary indulgence to all persons of either sex who make such a veneration for six consecutive Sundays. To be eligible for this plenary indulgence, the person must feel true penitence for their sins, they must receive the most Blessed Sacrament, and they must undertake particular prayers, meditations, or other acts of piety in veneration of Saint Aloysius Gonzaga and to the glory of God. Such persons shall be granted a full indulgence for the remission of all their sins according to the will of God.

This decree was made by me, the cardinal-prefect of the Sacred Congregation for Indulgences and Holy Relics, on the third day of October, 1739. His Holiness, [Pope Clement XII,] has granted his gracious consent, approval, and authorization for this decree on the eleventh day of December of the same year.

+ *Ludovicus Picus, cardinal-prefect*
of the Sacred Congregation for
Indulgences and Holy Relics

II. Decree or Declaration Concerning Plenary
Indulgences for Acts of Piety, Prayer, and Meditation
on Six Consecutive Sundays Made in Honor
of Saint Aloysius Gonzaga

Recently our holy pontiff [Pope Clement XII]—pursuant to the counsel of my humble self, as prefect of

the Sacred Congregation of Indulgences and Sacred
Relics—granted a plenary indulgence for all sins to the
faithful, including all truly penitent persons of either
sex, who undertook prayer, meditation, or other acts
of piety in honor of Saint Aloysius Gonzaga and to the
glory of God for six consecutive Sundays before the
feast of that saint, or any other six consecutive Sundays
in the year. The question has been raised about whether
this is to be understood as a single plenary indulgence
for the devotions made on all the six Sundays or six
separate plenary indulgences for the devotions made on
each of the consecutive Sundays. The question has been
communicated by me, the cardinal-prefect of the Sacred
Congregation of Indulgences and Sacred Relics, to His
Holiness [Pope Clement XII]. The pontiff has kindly
declared that—for the sake of promoting the devotion
of the people towards this wonderful saint, who has
procured so many temporal and spiritual benefits for
God's faithful—that a separate plenary indulgence is to
be granted for each of the six consecutive Sundays. His
Holiness has directed that this decision be expressed by
decree on this seventh day of January, 1740.

+ *Ludovicus Picus, cardinal-prefect*
of the Sacred Congregation for
Indulgences and Holy Relics

Prayer

*A prayer intention to be repeated on each of
the six Sundays before the reading of the meditation.*

O Saint Aloysius, graciously accept this veneration which I am humbly offering for six consecutive Sundays for the glory of God and of His most blessed Virgin Mother and for your own special honor.

I offer it, first of all, as an expression of gratitude for the particular benefits and graces conferred upon me and upon all your devotees.

I offer it also in the hope of your efficacious intercession to assist me in the cultivation of unblemished purity of mind and of body, in the avoidance of occasions for sin and all perils, physical and spiritual, and in the conscientious daily emendation of all my faults and defects.

May I attain progress in all the virtues, in piety, in obedience, and in the other Christian qualities I need to develop. Above all, may I advance in loving God with all my heart, all my soul, and all my strength. May I be ready to face death rather than to stray from the love of God, who alone is our highest good!

I implore also your kind intercession in achieving good results in all my endeavors and preserving health of mind and body. May I experience the assistance of God and His angels in all my needs, and may I achieve success in all my undertakings—insofar as they contribute to the greater glory of God and the salvation of my immortal soul.

With great confidence and faith I implore these things through your intercession, Saint Aloysius, for you are a powerful advocate for me in heaven. Pray for me to the Lord Jesus, to whom you are now a companion in the realms of eternal bliss! Pray for me to the Virgin Mary, the Queen of Heaven, to whom you are an adopted son through grace and devotion!

Graciously hear my prayers, holy Aloysius, and respond to them with merciful kindness. Amen.

Meditation for the First Sunday: The Preservation of Innocence

"Who shall ascend the mountain of the Lord, and who shall dwell in his holy place? The one with innocent hands and a clean heart."[1]

This verse from the Psalm teaches us that those who cultivate purity and integrity of body and mind shall ascend to the most intimate union with God, the most chaste Spouse of the soul. Such persons shall stand unshakeable in virtue and grace and shall never be moved from their holy commitment to purity by any impulse of the flesh or of the devil. These are the ones

---

[1] Psalm 14:1–2.

of whom it is written, "they shall see God"[2] and "will be like the angels of the Lord in heaven,"[3] where "they shall follow the Lamb."[4] There, adorned with the laurels of untarnished virginity, "they shall shine like the stars for all eternity."[5] O, how marvelous and glorious is the reward of innocence!

But we hold this treasure—the precious treasure of holy innocence—in fragile vessels of clay.[6] And, in proportion to the great fragility of the vessel, so must our solicitude for the protection and preservation of the treasure of innocence be the more diligent and unceasing.

O most chaste Jesus, radiant splendor and mirror of the eternal Light! Grant that I may always preserve my body in chastity and may please you with a pure heart.

Saint Aloysius guarded and preserved the precious treasure of holy innocence carefully and thoroughly. Hence, he came to be known as "an angel in human flesh," "a prince without a body," and an "angelic youth." He dreaded all forms of sin and even the slightest shadow of sin and vice, avoiding these like fearsome pitfalls. He was very strict in reprimanding and correcting himself,

---

[2]   Matthew 5:8.
[3]   Matthew 22:30.
[4]   Revelation 14:4.
[5]   Daniel 12:3.
[6]   See 2 Corinthians 4:7.

even for the slightest fault, with heartfelt tears and penitence. Thus it was his earnest endeavor to be ready to appear before the heavenly throne of judgment at any moment without the slightest trepidation or carrying the burden of any unrepented or unconfessed guilt.

At the age of nine, he pledged his perpetual virginity to God. This perfect virginity he bore with him as an unstained baptismal robe until he arrived at his mortal tomb. As the Sacred Congregation in Rome testified, when he was added to the canon of saints, "Never once did he suffer from an impure thought in his mind, nor was he ever tempted by impure urgings of the flesh."

O Saint Aloysius, angelic youth—draw us after yourself so that we may run in the path of your fragrant sanctity until we arrive at last in the kingdom of paradise!

Meditation for the Second Sunday: Devotion to the Eucharist

"The Lord is merciful, and leaves a memorial of his wondrous deeds. He is compassionate, and gives food to those who fear him."[7]

What is this food referred to in the verse above, which the Lord gives to those who fear Him? It is nothing other than the flesh assumed from the Virgin, the

---

[7] Psalm 110:4–5.

Bread of Angels, His only-begotten Son. How stupendous and incredible is this feast, which strikes even the minds of the angels with awe and wonder! To all those fearing Him is this holy food given, but this does not mean that we should have a servile or cowardly fear. For such a fear would prevent one from receiving the Blessed Sacrament frequently. But rather, the "fear" spoken of is a filial reverence and a fitting modesty and humility.

For the Lord sincerely desires the sacrament of His Body and Blood to be consumed by us, such as when He says, "Come to me, all ye who labor and are heavily burdened, and I shall refresh you."[8] Yet He also warns us against unworthy reception of the Eucharist in the Scripture, "Let each person examine themselves, and only then eat of this bread. For the one who receives it unworthily will be condemned through the Body and Blood of Christ."[9] Woe to the one who enters the wedding feast without wearing the appropriate garment![10]

Lord, I am not worthy that you should enter under my roof, but only say the word, and my soul shall be healed!

---

[8]   Matthew 11:28.
[9]   1 Corinthians 11:29.
[10] See Matthew 22:12.

How wonderfully prepared and splendidly clothed in the fitting raiment of virtue and reverence did Saint Aloysius approach the table of the divine wedding feast! It was Saint Charles Borromeo himself who instructed the angelic youth in the proper way of receiving the Eucharist. He always took three days to prepare himself spiritually for the reception of the sacrament, and then would spend the same number of days afterwards in giving thanks to God.[11] In the days of preparation, he would devote many hours to prayer and conversation with the Lord. For one day prior to receiving the Body and Blood of Christ, he would fast assiduously. When he did approach the Eucharistic table, it was with incredible modesty, reverence, fervor, and longing.

Nothing could be sweeter to him than to speak of, to read about, or to meditate upon this most holy Mystery. Nothing was more delightful to him than to be attentively present at the celebration of the Mass, in which the pure victim and holy sacrifice of the Lamb without blemish is offered as the price of our eternal redemption. And there was nothing he longed for more ardently than

---

[11] As previously noted, daily reception of the Eucharist was not a standard practice at the time, even amongst religious. Reception of the Blessed Sacrament once a week, or even once a month, would have been considered "frequent."

to gaze in loving adoration upon the Blessed Sacrament, in which all the radiant glory of the Divinity lies veiled under the appearances of mortal bread!

O most innocent seraph, blessed Aloysius—how earnestly I desire to consume in your company this wondrous and mystic Passover! Grant that my own heart may always burn with the same passionate fire as yours in loving Jesus Christ, truly present in the sacrament of the Holy Eucharist.

Meditation for the Third Sunday: Love for the Virgin Mary

"God wills us to possess all His gifts through Mary!"[12]

Truly, the Blessed Virgin is the channel through which all the gifts of celestial grace are poured out to us from the infinite ocean of divine goodness. If it is purity of heart we desire, it is Mary who shall bestow it upon us. If it is the blessing of good health, or success in one's studies, or clarity in times of doubts, or strength to resist temptations—all of these God desires to give to us through Mary. And she is not able to hear our tears and cries without being moved to compassion by them. For she is truly the mother of mercy, and, although we

---

[12] This sentence is attributed to Saint Bernard of Clairvaux.

are sinners, she embraces us in the arms of her maternal love. She is the clement, loving, and sweet Virgin who graciously turns unto us her eyes of mercy! And, after this exile of our earthly life, she will most surely show to us the blessed fruit of her womb, Jesus. For our part, all we must do is attempt to please her and her divine Son through integrity of heart and purity of body.

O most holy Virgin Queen, deign to accept my humble praise! Grant to me strength and fortitude wherewith to fight successfully against all my spiritual enemies and foes!

Saint Aloysius loved Mary as his spiritual mother with a most tender and filial affection. Indeed, his whole heart was taken up in her love whenever he thought of her. This included whenever he spoke of her with his peers, or saw a sacred image of her, or heard, read, or wrote her holy name, or happened to read some work of pious devotion concerning her. This was a very frequent experience for him and always brought to him an unspeakably sweet sensation of delight.

He was constant in his daily recitation of the Office of Our Lady once he had commenced this practice[13] and never once omitted it, even when afflicted with

---

[13] Aloysius began the daily praying of the Office of Our Lady at the age of seven.

serious illness. He would say this either at home at a small altar he had set up to the Blessed Virgin or at any Marian shrine or altar, and always with tears and sighs of devotion and love. Whenever he had some particular need for solace, guidance, or help, he would beseech the Mother of God in prayer. He would say an Ave, echoing the angel Gabriel's greeting of Mary, with almost every step he took, and particularly when he was walking up stairs. It was his custom to recite silently various Marian litanies and rosaries in any unoccupied moment, and all feast days of Our Lady he observed with particular solemnity and reverence. He also made a diligent effort to emulate the virtues of the holy Virgin, especially her modesty, meekness, obedience, and innocence, and would frequently speak of these same virtues with passionate enthusiasm to his peers.

Oh, if only I could also be like that! Grant, O most holy Aloysius, that I may come to reflect something of the example of your piety, love, and constancy in my own devotions to the holy Mother of our glorious Savior.

Meditation for the Fourth Sunday: Self-Denial

"Those who belong to Christ, crucify their self-indulgent tendencies and vices. Learn to deny yourself, to cast off the 'old man,' to discipline the body, and thus to make it the servant of the soul, not its master!"[14]

The counsel given above by Saint Paul truly is of Christ. It conforms to Christ's teaching and, furthermore, expresses a principle that was exhibited in the example of Christ's own life. Consider that Jesus was the one who is rightfully our divine Lord and Master and yet who, in humility, lay in swaddling clothes in a manger, who fled to Egypt as an exile, who obeyed Mary and Joseph in their simple house in Nazareth, and who fasted for forty long days and nights in the solitude of the desert. Consider Him also laboring to preach the Gospel and finally dying upon the cross for our sins. What is the life of Jesus but an example and model of continual self-denial and mastery of the desires of the flesh and heart? Let us strive to imitate Our Lord and Teacher in doing this!

O Lord, I do not wish to live surrounded by delicacies and luxuries when You, the Head of the Church,

---

[14] See Galatians 5:24.

underwent constant privations and hardships! Help me to be conformed to Your example and to become more like You, who accepted even the suffering of the cross.

This, indeed, is exactly what blessed Aloysius did in his own life. He declared that "no one has ever attained to the apex of spiritual perfection unless he regards his body as a mere servant of the soul—a beast of labor, which must be tamed, subdued, and commanded."

One of the ways in which Aloysius exercised such self-denial was his austerity in matters of food. He ate no more than was sufficient for maintaining his well-being and always abstained from desserts and treats which are eaten merely for pleasure, not for nutrition.

Furthermore, he would often spend long hours of the night kneeling in prayer, even during the cold months of winter. Moreover, whatever he suffered due to illness or disease, he endured with uncomplaining and invincible patience. Even before he commenced his religious life with the Jesuits and still resided in his noble father's splendid palace, he lived a life of self-denial and austerity which exceeded that of most professed religious.

O Aloysius, unknown martyr—teach me to discipline and restrain the impulses of my body while I am on earth: to die to the flesh so that I may live in the spirit!

Meditation for the Fifth Sunday:
Control of the Senses

"Let your modesty be known to all people."[15]

The internal character of a person is generally readily perceived through their external control of the senses. Those who have inner tranquility and discipline will naturally restrain the movements and wanderings of their eyes, tongue, and hands. The one who possesses angelic virtue and innocence will always be recognized as such, for this virtue will manifest itself in modesty and serenity of demeanor and control and restraint of the senses. And the development of this heavenly virtue is most necessary for all those who desire to approach the angels in their realm of glory and bliss through purity of heart and body.

Chastity and charity are the companions of true modesty, and they are all fruits of the same Holy Spirit. But no one can retain chastity for long if they allow the enemy of the soul to enter through the doors and windows of the external senses. Indeed, this is how the devil breaks into the house of one's heart to steal away its precious treasure! He enters through the windows of the eyes and ears and then seizes the gold of innocence

---

[15] Philippians 4:5.

and steals it away. We have all seen this happen to many people. My friend, let the dangers which have overcome so many others make you cautious!

O Lord, place a guard around my mouth and a door against my lips[16] so that I may not stray from the path of modesty and wander into the ways of iniquity and licentiousness!

We have an example of angelic modesty in Saint Aloysius. For he was restrained in his speech, grave and dignified in his step, serene in the expression he bore on his face, cautious in directing his eyes, and like an angel in all his physical movements. The eyes are the first seat of modesty, and of these he diligently kept custody, not allowing his glance to stray around purposelessly or out of curiosity. This he did to such an extent that there were those who knew him for three years or more without ever observing the color of his eyes. And he never paid attention to public spectacles or displays of royal magnificence, or theatrical entertainments; rather, he either kept his eyes fixed on the ground or contemplated the image of celestial realities in his mind. And just as he so kept disciplined custody over his eyes, so did Aloysius control the movements

---

[16] See Psalm 140:3.

of his hand and tongue. Indeed, he was unvaryingly mature, grave, and circumspect in all his actions.

Most modest Aloysius—teach me not to let my eyes wander vainly, to close my ears to hearing wicked and foolish things, and to restrain my tongue from saying what is imprudent! Doing thus, may I come to resemble you in your sanctity and self-control and the holy angels in their ineffable serenity and peace.

Meditation for the Sixth Sunday: A Holy Manner of Living

"We shall be seen in the sight of the entire universe—both the angels and all humankind."[17]

If we diligently practice a holy manner of living, we shall serve as a correction and call to emendation to the world. We shall also be a delight in the sight of the angels. And we shall profit all humankind by offering an edifying example. When the wicked world witnesses the justice and innocence of our actions, they shall be alerted to their own errors and made aware of their own depravity. When the angels see us imitating their innocence and purity, they shall be refreshed and filled with joy and satisfaction. And when, by our actions

---

[17] 1 Corinthians 4:9.

and behavior, we are able to excite the ardor of piety in the hearts of our fellow human beings, we shall surely edify them in the Lord.

How much merit shall we gain if, by means of our example, brothers and sisters who are straying from the straight and narrow path of faith should be diverted from the harmful error of false worldly liberty! What exultation shall there be in heaven if, in our peace, charity, and meekness, we are seen to grow to resemble the angelic spirits! And who will not be encouraged in the pursuit of virtue if we are able to offer to them the good example of a holy and chaste life?

Lord, let our light shine in the presence of all people so that they may see our good works and glorify our Father who is in heaven![18]

Thus, indeed, did Aloysius shine forth in his family's palace while engaged in studies, in times of recreation, and in all forms of society. In each situation and setting, he exhibited perfect sanctity, innocence, and circumspection. Many of his fellow aristocrats marveled that a mere youth should exhibit such gravity, maturity, and restraint of speech. Many of his fellow students were amazed to see such assiduity, affability,

---

[18] See Matthew 5:16.

and obedience. Many of his confreres in the religious life were astounded by his zeal, humility, and careful observance of all rules and regulations.

He avoided consorting with members of the opposite sex lest he fall into lust, temptation, or distraction. And he always fled from parties, feasts, and theatrical entertainments. Furthermore, he was extremely prudent in choosing his friends, selecting none but those who were diligent and zealous in their piety and industrious in their literary, philosophical, and theological studies. His delight was always in holy and edifying speech, and he abhorred flippant jesting, licentious comments, and dissipated conversation of any kind.

O most self-controlled and holy Aloysius—grant that I may be led by your wonderful example and make my pilgrimage through this fleeting world in such a way that my heart is always fixed longingly on heaven and my conduct authentically reflects this celestial desire.

And may I one day arrive in that glorious realm of bliss—the supernal, star-illumined city of eternal beatitude—to rejoice there forever with you, with the Blessed Virgin Mary, with all the holy angels and saints, and with their immortal King, Our Lord Jesus Christ, who lives and reigns with the Father and the Holy Spirit, God forever and ever! Amen.